THE BEST
ADULT
WORLD RECORDS

meadowside
CHILDREN'S BOOKS

LARGEST CONDOM

A 21.94 m (72 ft) condom was fitted over the Obelisque in Place de la Concorde, Paris, France, on 1 December 1993 to mark World AIDS Day. The condom was funded by Italian clothes firm Benetton.

LARGEST NATURAL BREASTS

Annie Hawkins-Turner (aka Norma Stitz) has an under-breast measurement of 109.22 cm (43 in) and an around-chest-over-nipple measurement of 177.8 cm (70 in). She currently wears a US size 52I bra.

LARGEST REPRODUCTIVE ORGAN

The largest reproductive organ of any living creature belongs to the Giant Sperm Whale (*Physeter catodon*) whose retractable penis can be up to 2 m (6.5 ft) long. The peak of the mating season is in the spring in both northern and southern hemispheres, so most calves are born in the autumn.

OLDEST MALE STRIPPER

Bernie Barker was born on 31 July 1940 and is a regular performer at Club LeBare, Miami Beach, Florida, USA. He began his career in 2000 at the age of 60 as a way to get in shape after recovering from prostate cancer. Since leaving his previous job of selling real estate, he has won over 30 contests.

HEAVIEST MODEL

American model Teighlor reached a peak weight of 326.14 kg (718.7 lb) in the early 1990s and has forged a successful modelling career, appearing in films, on greetings cards and in advertisements.

MOST SEX CHANGE OPERATIONS PERFORMED

Surgeon Stanley Biber has performed sex change operations for over 30 years in Trinidad, Colorado, USA. The three-hour operation costs approximately £18,750. He has conducted 3,000 male-to-female operations and about 250 female-to-male operations.

MOST PLASTIC SURGERY

Fulvia Celica Siguas Sandoval (Peru) has had 64 cosmetic operations since December 1979. Of these, over 25 have been to her face and neck, with her other alterations including ear reductions, transformations to her legs, and arm liposuction.

OLDEST LOVE MANUAL

Vatsyayana's *Kama Sutra* is believed to be the oldest love and sex manual in existence. Generally considered the standard work on love in Sanskrit literature, the book is thought to have been written sometime in the fourth century AD. Today, the *Kama Sutra* is widely available and has been translated into a number of languages. There are 35 chapters in total, and only one refers to sex. The rest concern social customs, mores, love, philosophy and spirituality.

GREATEST NUMBER OF DESCENDANTS

At the time of his death on 15 October 1992, Samuel S Mast, aged 96, of Fryburg, Pennsylvania, USA, had 824 living descendants. The roll call comprised 11 children, 97 grandchildren, 634 great-grandchildren and 82 great-great-grandchildren. The last Sharifian Emperor of Morocco, Moulay Ismail (1672–1727), known as The Bloodthirsty, was reputed to have fathered a total of 525 sons and 342 daughters by 1703 and achieved a 700th son in 1721.

MOST EXPENSIVE BRA

The 'Red Hot Fantasy' bra, created by Victoria's Secret, is the latest in a line of luxury lingerie Christmas gifts. Priced at £10 million, the fiery-red bra contains over 1,300 precious stones, including 300 carats of ravishing Thai rubies set among dazzling diamonds.

LONGEST BRA CHAIN

Organized by Class 95FM, Wacoal and the Breast Cancer Foundation for Breast Cancer Awareness, the world's longest bra chain consisted of 79,001 bras, and measured 60.015 km (37.5 miles) on Sentosa Island, Singapore, on 21 December 2002.

LARGEST BRA

In September 1990, Triumph International Japan Ltd developed a brassiere with an underbust measurement of 24 m (78 ft 8 in) and a bust measurement of 28 m (91 ft 10 in). The bra is based on the Tyrolean Cut (underwired ³/₄ cup), which Triumph introduced in 1970. It was made from 70 m (229 ft) of fabric, enough to make 1,000 'regular' bras.

GREATEST AGE DIFFERENCE FOR A MARRIED COUPLE

Gertrude Grubb (b. 3 July 1909) was 18 when she married 81-year-old Union Civil War veteran John Janeway – an age difference of 63 years. The last Union widow of an American Civil War veteran, she died on 17 January 2003 aged 93.

GREATEST WEIGHT DIFFERENTIAL FOR A MARRIED COUPLE

The greatest weight differential recorded for a married couple is c. 585 kg (1,289.7 lb), in the case of Jon Brower Minnoch and his 50 kg (110.2 lb) wife Jeanette (both USA). Once the heaviest man in the world, Jon weighed approximately 635 kg (1,397 lb). The couple were married in March 1978 and had two sons.

MOST NATIONALITIES IN A SAUNA

On 8 March 2002, in Halmstad, Sweden, 29 participants from 29 different countries crammed into the same sauna and shut the door for 10 min – setting the record for most nationalities simultaneously in a sauna.

COSTLIEST E-MAIL

In 1997, a subsidiary of US-based petroleum company Chevron Corp paid £1.3 million to settle a sexual-harassment lawsuit filed against it by four female employees. Evidence presented by the women's lawyers included an e-mail listing 25 reasons why beer is supposedly better than women. In settling, Chevron denied the women's allegations.

MOST GENDER-AWARE ROBOT

Artificial intelligence company Intelligent Earth (Kirkcaldy, UK) has developed visual gender recognition software for its robotic head 'Doki'. Based on visual data alone, Doki can recognize the gender of women with an accuracy of 100%, and men with an accuracy of 96%. Doki is also able to scientifically rate the attractiveness of women.

LARGEST G-STRING

The world's largest g-string was unveiled at the Body Shop's UK headquarters in Littlehampton, West Sussex, on 15 March 2001. The giant white and red cotton thong measured approximately 9.2 x 4.6 m (30 x 15 ft), and was produced by the Body Shop in conjunction with Comic Relief's 'Pants to Poverty' campaign.

LARGEST NUDE PHOTO SHOOT

A total of 7,000 people volunteered to pose collectively in the nude on a street in Barcelona, Spain, for photographer Spencer Tunick (USA) on 8 June 2003.

LARGEST UNDERPANTS

The world's largest pair of cotton underwear measured 9.54 m (31.29 ft) wide and 4.9 m (16 ft) tall and was created by the Exeter Council for Voluntary Service and unveiled on 7 June 2003 at the Exeter County Rugby Ground, Devon, UK.

MOST CASES OF SEXUALLY TRANSMITTED DISEASE INFECTIONS

In 1995, the World Health Organization (WHO) estimated that there were a record 333 million new cases of the four most common curable sexually transmitted infections (STIs) – gonorrhea, chlamydia, syphilis and trichomonas.

LONGEST RUNNING THEATRICAL COMEDY

The longest running comedy was *No Sex Please: We're British*, written by Anthony Marriott and Alistair Foot (both UK) and presented by John Gale (UK). It opened at the Strand Theatre on 3 June 1971, transferred to the Duchess Theatre on 2 August 1986, and finally ended on 5 September 1987 after 16 years 3 months and 6,761 performances.

MOST FERTILE ANIMAL

It has been calculated that with unlimited food and no predators, a single cabbage aphid (*Brevicoryne brassicae*) could theoretically give rise in a year to a mass of descendants weighing 822 million tonnes, or more than three times the total weight of the world's human population.

MOST DANGEROUS LOVE LIFE

The male brown antechinus (*Antechinus stuartii*), a marsupial mouse that inhabits eastern Australia, has an insatiable sexual appetite. Every year, the entire adult male population goes on a rampage for two weeks in a desperate bid to mate with as many females as possible. It is believed that the heightened stress levels from chasing females and fighting off rival males shuts down the immune system, and all die within a matter of days owing to ulcers or infection – or starvation, as they also neglect to eat.

LARGEST REPRODUCTIVE ORGAN FOR A BIRD

The largest penis of any bird is that of the Argentinean lake drake (*Oxyura vittata*) which has been measured everted and unwound at 42.5 cm (16.7 in). The base of this retractable penis is covered with spines, yet the tip is soft and brush-like.

OLDEST BEER

Written references to beer have been found dating from as far back as c. 5000 BC, as part of the daily wages of workers at the Temple of Erech in Mesopotamia. Physical evidence of beer dating from c. 3500 BC was detected in remains of a jug found at Godin Tepe, Iran, in 1973 during a Royal Ontario Museum expedition.

LARGEST SHOT SLAM

The largest shot slam took place at Bath University, Bath, UK, on 21 March 2002. The attempt consisted of 749 members of BUMS (Bath University Maths Society), who all downed tequila.

MOST PUBS VISITED

Bruce Masters of Flitwick, Bedfordshire, UK, has visited 31,751 pubs and a further 1,974 other drinking establishments since 1960, partaking of the local brew in each case where available.

LARGEST ALCOHOL CONSUMERS

According to surveys done in 2000, the country with the largest annual per capita consumption of alcohol is Ireland, with 12.3 litres (21.6 pints) of pure alcohol per person. This intake is based on the amount of pure alcohol consumed within wine, beer and spirits. Luxembourg comes in at second place with 12.1 litres (21.2 pints) per person, followed by Romania with 11.7 litres (20.5 pints) per person.

LARGEST SPIRITS CONSUMERS

Russia has the highest annual consumption of spirits per person, with every Russian consuming on average 4.4 litres (7.7 pints) of pure alcohol in 1994.

HIGHEST BLOOD ALCOHOL LEVEL

The University of California Medical School, Los Angeles, USA, reported in December 1982 the case of a confused but conscious 24-year-old female who was shown to have a blood alcohol level of 1,510 mg per 100 ml – nearly 19 times the UK driving limit (80 mg of alcohol per 100 ml of blood) and triple the normally lethal limit. She discharged herself after just two days!

STRONGEST BEER COMMERCIALLY AVAILABLE

The strongest beer commercially available is Sam Adams Utopias MM II, which is brewed by the Boston Beer Company, Massachusetts, USA, and has an alcohol volume of 24%.

FASTEST TIME TO DRINK A PINT OF STOUT

Peter Dowdeswell of Earls Barton, Northamptonshire, drank a pint of stout in 2.1 sec at Millwall Football Club, London, UK, on 24 April 2001.

HIGHEST CONSUMPTION PER CAPITA

The Czech Republic is the leading beer consumer per capita, with 160 litres (281.56 pints) per person per year as of 2000. This is followed by Ireland with 152 litres (267.5 pints) per capita, and Germany with 125.5 litres (220.8 pints) per capita.

FASTEST TIME TO DRINK A PINT OF BEER UPSIDE DOWN

The UK's Peter Dowdeswell drank a pint of beer while standing on his head in 3 sec at BBC Radio Leicester studios, UK, on 16 February 1988.

LOWEST SUICIDE RATE

Antigua and Barbuda (1995), the Dominican Republic (1994), Saint Kitts and Nevis (1995), and Saint Vincent and The Grenadines (1986) have all recorded the lowest suicide rates with no cases reported in the years shown.

GREATEST MASS SUICIDE

As reported by the Roman historian Flavius Josephus, some 960 Jewish zealots committed suicide by cutting each other's throats at Masada, Israel, in AD 73, as the palace was being besieged by Romans. The men killed all the women and children, and then drew lots to select ten men. These ten slew all the other men, and then drew lots to choose one man. This man, in turn, killed the other nine before falling on his own sword.

HIGHEST ROAD FATALITY RATE

India's roads are rated as the most dangerous in the world. The country contains only 1% of the world's road vehicles but accounts for 6% of its road accidents. Of the 9.34 million deaths in India in 1998, 217,000 or 1 in 43 were as a result of road traffic accidents.

LONGEST WORKING GRAVEDIGGER

It is recorded that Johann Heinrich Karl Thieme, sexton of Aldenburg, Germany, dug 23,311 graves during a 50-year career. In 1826, his understudy dug Johann's grave.

SHORTEST REIGN EVER

The Crown Prince Luis Filipe of Portugal
was technically King of Portugal for about
20 min on 1 February 1908. His father was
shot in the streets of Lisbon and killed by a
bullet that severed his carotid artery, and
the Crown Prince was mortally wounded at
the same time.

MOST FATAL ATTACKS BY A WOLF

A wild wolf called the 'Beast of Gevauden' attacked dozens of children and adults in the mountainous region of Lozere, France, over a period of two years. More than 100 wolves were killed before the killer wolf was shot on 19 January 1766. When it was cut open, the shoulder of a young child killed the previous day was found inside its stomach.

EARLIEST LEGAL EUTHANASIA

The first person to end his life by legally sanctioned euthanasia was Ben Dent of Darwin, Australia, on 22 September 1996. He had been suffering from cancer for five years and died with the aid of a computerized death machine.

MOST EXPENSIVE HOTEL SUITE

The most expensive hotel room in the world is the Imperial Suite at the President Wilson Hotel in Geneva, Switzerland, which can be reserved for CHF45,000 (£20,907) per night. The suite, which is accessed by a private elevator, takes up an entire floor and has four bedrooms all of which overlook Lake Geneva. The dining room seats 26 guests and the living room can comfortably hold 40 people.
All windows and doors to the suite are bulletproof.

LONGEST CIGAR

On 18 April 2001, Jose Castelar Cairo
unveiled a cigar he hand-rolled himself over
nine days measuring 11.04 m (36.2 ft) long
at 'La Triada', Tiendas Habana Universo
Cubanacan S.A., Havana, Cuba.

MOST DRIVING OFFENCES

On 27 November 1975, John Hogg, at the High Court in Edinburgh, Scotland, received 5 years 9 months in jail and his third, fourth and fifth life bans for drunken driving in a stolen car while disqualified. He had 40 previous offences, for which he had received bans of 718 years plus two life bans.

MOST EXPENSIVE COFFEE

The most expensive coffee in the world is
Kopi Luwak coffee, which sells for
approximately £215 per pound (0.45 kg).
This is partly due to the fact that there is
only 227 kg (500 lb) of it available every
year. However, the price also reflects the
manner in which it is processed. The beans
are collected from the excrement of the
Sumatran civet cat (*Paradoxurus*). The civet
climbs into the coffee trees and eats the ripest
coffee cherries it can find. Eventually, these
reappear in the animal's excrement and are
gathered by locals.

HEAVIEST SMOKERS

South Korea has the highest per capita consumption of cigarettes anywhere in the world, at 4,153 units per annum. According to the World Health Organization, an estimated 4.6 trillion cigarettes were smoked in 1999. Figures from 2002 reveal that approximately 15 billion cigarettes are sold daily around the world, which works out to 10 million per minute.

For even **more**
fascinating
facts...

100s of
new
records!
ALL NEW
pictures!

www.guinnessworldrecords.com

Cartoons by:
Guy Harvey

Designed and edited by:
Jon Richards, Ed Simkins

For Guinness World Records:
Claire Folkard, Craig Glenday,
Kim Lacey, Christian Marais

Printed in India

The cartoons in this book are not intended to depict or refer to any real person, living or dead.